# How to Draw UNICORNS

THIS BOOK
BELONGS TO :

_______________________________

_______________________________

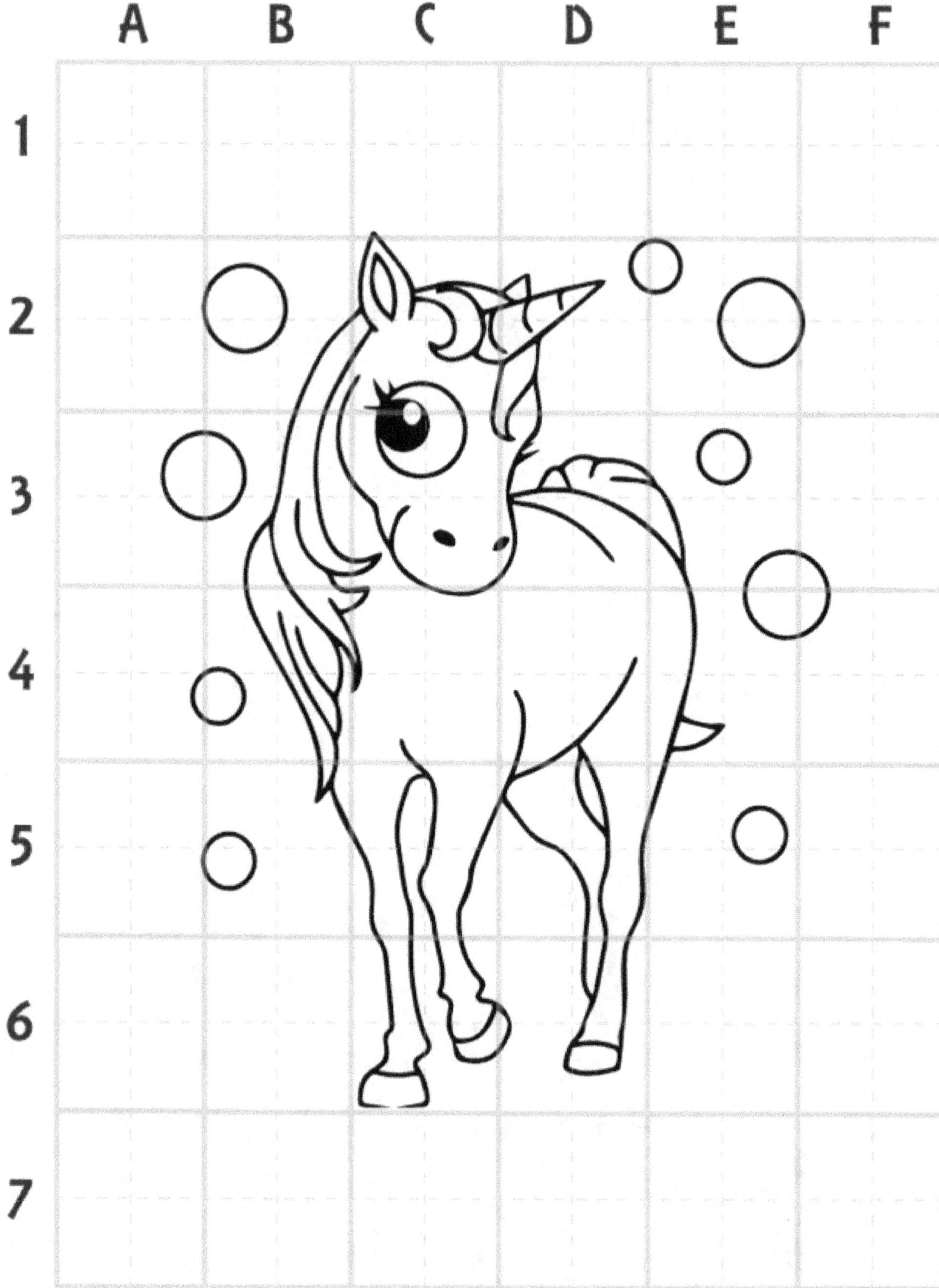

# YOUR TURN!

|   | A | B | C | D | E | F |
|---|---|---|---|---|---|---|
| 1 |   |   |   |   |   |   |
| 2 |   |   |   |   |   |   |
| 3 |   |   |   |   |   |   |
| 4 |   |   |   |   |   |   |
| 5 |   |   |   |   |   |   |
| 6 |   |   |   |   |   |   |
| 7 |   |   |   |   |   |   |

A    B    C    D    E    F
1
2
3
4
5
6
7

# YOUR TURN!

|   | A | B | C | D | E | F |
|---|---|---|---|---|---|---|
| 1 |   |   |   |   |   |   |
| 2 |   |   |   |   |   |   |
| 3 |   |   |   |   |   |   |
| 4 |   |   |   |   |   |   |
| 5 |   |   |   |   |   |   |
| 6 |   |   |   |   |   |   |
| 7 |   |   |   |   |   |   |

|  | A | B | C | D | E | F |
|---|---|---|---|---|---|---|
| 1 | | | | | | |
| 2 | | | | | | |
| 3 | | | | | | |
| 4 | | | | | | |
| 5 | | | | | | |
| 6 | | | | | | |
| 7 | | | | | | |

# YOUR TURN!

|   | A | B | C | D | E | F |
|---|---|---|---|---|---|---|
| 1 |   |   |   |   |   |   |
| 2 |   |   |   |   |   |   |
| 3 |   |   |   |   |   |   |
| 4 |   |   |   |   |   |   |
| 5 |   |   |   |   |   |   |
| 6 |   |   |   |   |   |   |
| 7 |   |   |   |   |   |   |

# YOUR TURN!

|  | A | B | C | D | E | F |
|---|---|---|---|---|---|---|
| 1 |  |  |  |  |  |  |
| 2 |  |  |  |  |  |  |
| 3 |  |  |  |  |  |  |
| 4 |  |  |  |  |  |  |
| 5 |  |  |  |  |  |  |
| 6 |  |  |  |  |  |  |
| 7 |  |  |  |  |  |  |

|     | A | B | C | D | E | F |
|-----|---|---|---|---|---|---|
| 1   |   |   |   |   |   |   |
| 2   |   |   |   |   |   |   |
| 3   |   |   |   |   |   |   |
| 4   |   |   |   |   |   |   |
| 5   |   |   |   |   |   |   |
| 6   |   |   |   |   |   |   |
| 7   |   |   |   |   |   |   |

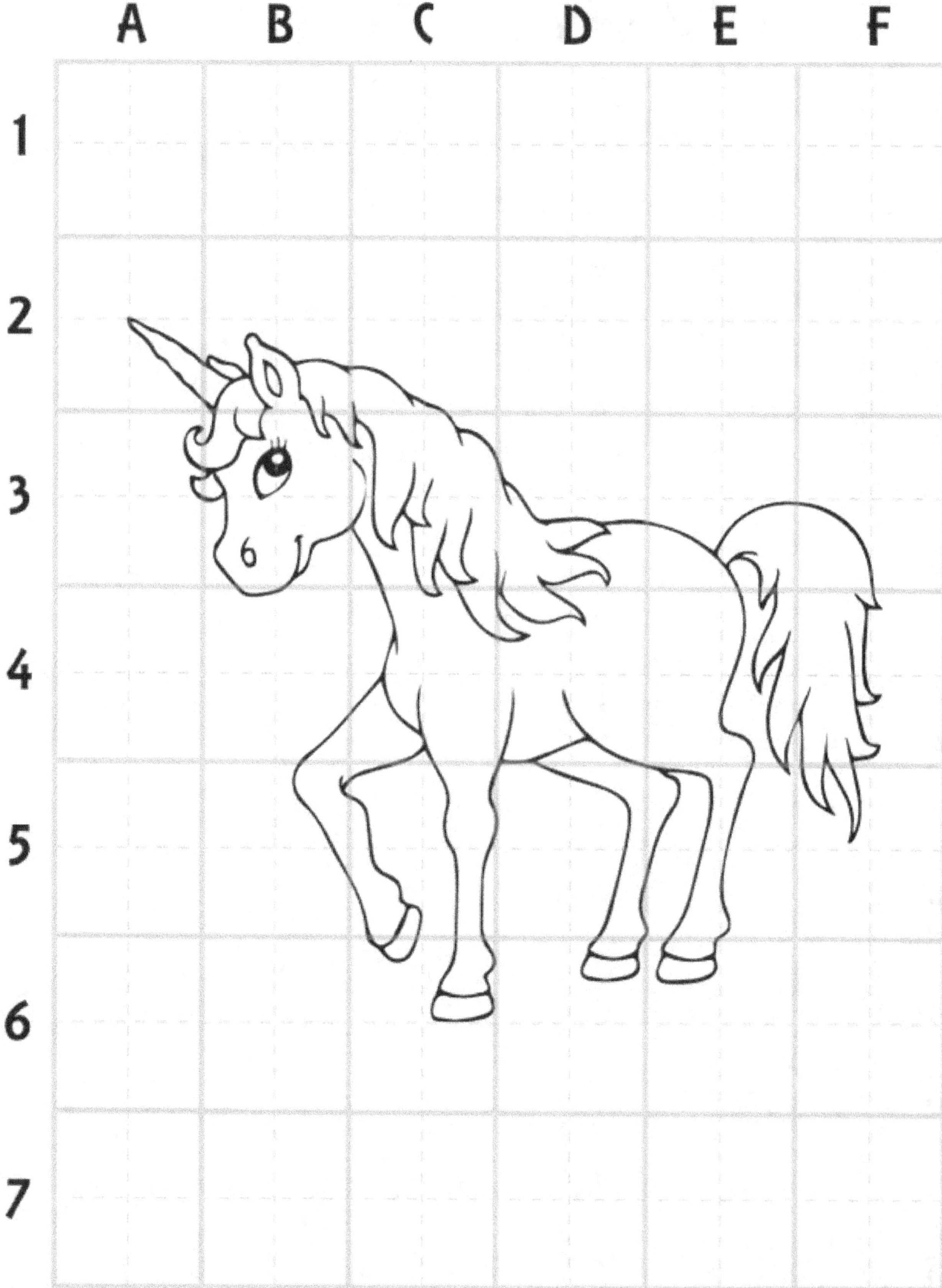

# YOUR TURN!

|   | A | B | C | D | E | F |
|---|---|---|---|---|---|---|
| 1 |   |   |   |   |   |   |
| 2 |   |   |   |   |   |   |
| 3 |   |   |   |   |   |   |
| 4 |   |   |   |   |   |   |
| 5 |   |   |   |   |   |   |
| 6 |   |   |   |   |   |   |
| 7 |   |   |   |   |   |   |

A    B    C    D    E    F
1
2
3
4
5
6
7

# YOUR TURN!

|   | A | B | C | D | E | F |
|---|---|---|---|---|---|---|
| 1 |   |   |   |   |   |   |
| 2 |   |   |   |   |   |   |
| 3 |   |   |   |   |   |   |
| 4 |   |   |   |   |   |   |
| 5 |   |   |   |   |   |   |
| 6 |   |   |   |   |   |   |
| 7 |   |   |   |   |   |   |

A B C D E F
1
2
3
4
5
6
7

# YOUR TURN!

|   | A | B | C | D | E | F |
|---|---|---|---|---|---|---|
| 1 |   |   |   |   |   |   |
| 2 |   |   |   |   |   |   |
| 3 |   |   |   |   |   |   |
| 4 |   |   |   |   |   |   |
| 5 |   |   |   |   |   |   |
| 6 |   |   |   |   |   |   |
| 7 |   |   |   |   |   |   |

A    B    C    D    E    F
1
2
3
4
5
6
7

# YOUR TURN!

|   | A | B | C | D | E | F |
|---|---|---|---|---|---|---|
| 1 |   |   |   |   |   |   |
| 2 |   |   |   |   |   |   |
| 3 |   |   |   |   |   |   |
| 4 |   |   |   |   |   |   |
| 5 |   |   |   |   |   |   |
| 6 |   |   |   |   |   |   |
| 7 |   |   |   |   |   |   |

# YOUR TURN!

|   | A | B | C | D | E | F |
|---|---|---|---|---|---|---|
| 1 |   |   |   |   |   |   |
| 2 |   |   |   |   |   |   |
| 3 |   |   |   |   |   |   |
| 4 |   |   |   |   |   |   |
| 5 |   |   |   |   |   |   |
| 6 |   |   |   |   |   |   |
| 7 |   |   |   |   |   |   |

A  B  C  D  E  F
1
2
3
4
5
6
7

# YOUR TURN!

|   | A | B | C | D | E | F |
|---|---|---|---|---|---|---|
| 1 |   |   |   |   |   |   |
| 2 |   |   |   |   |   |   |
| 3 |   |   |   |   |   |   |
| 4 |   |   |   |   |   |   |
| 5 |   |   |   |   |   |   |
| 6 |   |   |   |   |   |   |
| 7 |   |   |   |   |   |   |

# YOUR TURN!

|   | A | B | C | D | E | F |
|---|---|---|---|---|---|---|
| 1 |   |   |   |   |   |   |
| 2 |   |   |   |   |   |   |
| 3 |   |   |   |   |   |   |
| 4 |   |   |   |   |   |   |
| 5 |   |   |   |   |   |   |
| 6 |   |   |   |   |   |   |
| 7 |   |   |   |   |   |   |

A B C D E F
1
2
3
4
5
6
7

# YOUR TURN!

|   | A | B | C | D | E | F |
|---|---|---|---|---|---|---|
| 1 |   |   |   |   |   |   |
| 2 |   |   |   |   |   |   |
| 3 |   |   |   |   |   |   |
| 4 |   |   |   |   |   |   |
| 5 |   |   |   |   |   |   |
| 6 |   |   |   |   |   |   |
| 7 |   |   |   |   |   |   |

A    B    C    D    E    F
1
2
3
4
5
6
7

# YOUR TURN!

|   | A | B | C | D | E | F |
|---|---|---|---|---|---|---|
| 1 |   |   |   |   |   |   |
| 2 |   |   |   |   |   |   |
| 3 |   |   |   |   |   |   |
| 4 |   |   |   |   |   |   |
| 5 |   |   |   |   |   |   |
| 6 |   |   |   |   |   |   |
| 7 |   |   |   |   |   |   |

A  B  C  D  E  F
1
2
3
4
5
6
7

# YOUR TURN!

|   | A | B | C | D | E | F |
|---|---|---|---|---|---|---|
| 1 |   |   |   |   |   |   |
| 2 |   |   |   |   |   |   |
| 3 |   |   |   |   |   |   |
| 4 |   |   |   |   |   |   |
| 5 |   |   |   |   |   |   |
| 6 |   |   |   |   |   |   |
| 7 |   |   |   |   |   |   |

A B C D E F
1
2
3
4
5
6
7

# YOUR TURN!

|  | A | B | C | D | E | F |
|---|---|---|---|---|---|---|
| 1 |  |  |  |  |  |  |
| 2 |  |  |  |  |  |  |
| 3 |  |  |  |  |  |  |
| 4 |  |  |  |  |  |  |
| 5 |  |  |  |  |  |  |
| 6 |  |  |  |  |  |  |
| 7 |  |  |  |  |  |  |

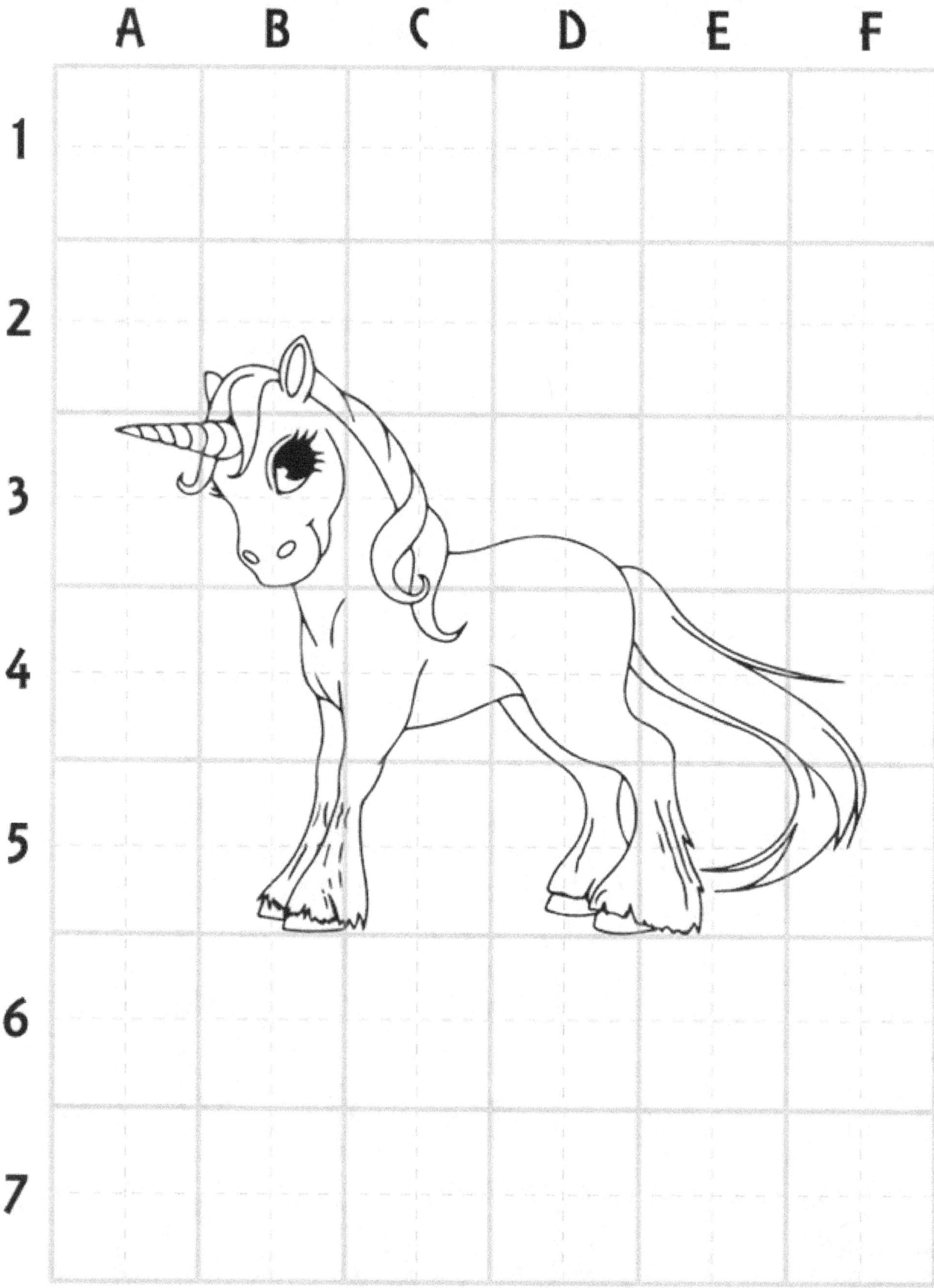

# YOUR TURN!

|   | A | B | C | D | E | F |
|---|---|---|---|---|---|---|
| 1 |   |   |   |   |   |   |
| 2 |   |   |   |   |   |   |
| 3 |   |   |   |   |   |   |
| 4 |   |   |   |   |   |   |
| 5 |   |   |   |   |   |   |
| 6 |   |   |   |   |   |   |
| 7 |   |   |   |   |   |   |

A B C D E F
1
2
3
4
5
6
7


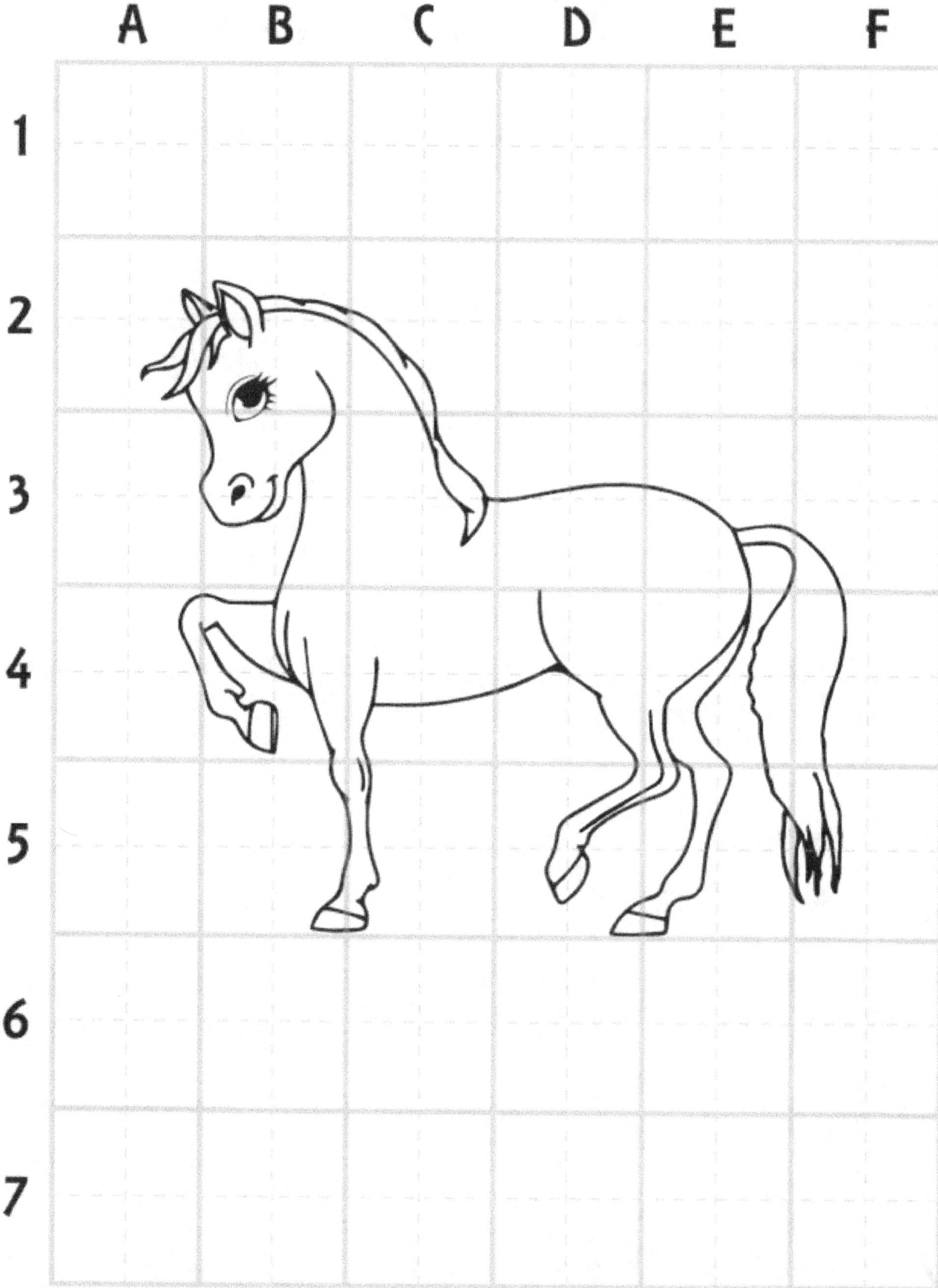

# YOUR TURN!

|   | A | B | C | D | E | F |
|---|---|---|---|---|---|---|
| 1 |   |   |   |   |   |   |
| 2 |   |   |   |   |   |   |
| 3 |   |   |   |   |   |   |
| 4 |   |   |   |   |   |   |
| 5 |   |   |   |   |   |   |
| 6 |   |   |   |   |   |   |
| 7 |   |   |   |   |   |   |

A B C D E F
1
2
3
4
5
6
7

# YOUR TURN!

|  | A | B | C | D | E | F |
|---|---|---|---|---|---|---|
| 1 |  |  |  |  |  |  |
| 2 |  |  |  |  |  |  |
| 3 |  |  |  |  |  |  |
| 4 |  |  |  |  |  |  |
| 5 |  |  |  |  |  |  |
| 6 |  |  |  |  |  |  |
| 7 |  |  |  |  |  |  |

A B C D E F
1
2
3
4
5
6
7

# YOUR TURN!

|   | A | B | C | D | E | F |
|---|---|---|---|---|---|---|
| 1 |   |   |   |   |   |   |
| 2 |   |   |   |   |   |   |
| 3 |   |   |   |   |   |   |
| 4 |   |   |   |   |   |   |
| 5 |   |   |   |   |   |   |
| 6 |   |   |   |   |   |   |
| 7 |   |   |   |   |   |   |

A    B    C    D    E    F
1
2
3
4
5
6
7

# YOUR TURN!

|   | A | B | C | D | E | F |
|---|---|---|---|---|---|---|
| 1 |   |   |   |   |   |   |
| 2 |   |   |   |   |   |   |
| 3 |   |   |   |   |   |   |
| 4 |   |   |   |   |   |   |
| 5 |   |   |   |   |   |   |
| 6 |   |   |   |   |   |   |
| 7 |   |   |   |   |   |   |

A    B    C    D    E    F

# YOUR TURN!

|   | A | B | C | D | E | F |
|---|---|---|---|---|---|---|
| 1 |   |   |   |   |   |   |
| 2 |   |   |   |   |   |   |
| 3 |   |   |   |   |   |   |
| 4 |   |   |   |   |   |   |
| 5 |   |   |   |   |   |   |
| 6 |   |   |   |   |   |   |
| 7 |   |   |   |   |   |   |

# YOUR TURN!

|   | A | B | C | D | E | F |
|---|---|---|---|---|---|---|
| 1 |   |   |   |   |   |   |
| 2 |   |   |   |   |   |   |
| 3 |   |   |   |   |   |   |
| 4 |   |   |   |   |   |   |
| 5 |   |   |   |   |   |   |
| 6 |   |   |   |   |   |   |
| 7 |   |   |   |   |   |   |

A B C D E F
1
2
3
4
5
6
7

# YOUR TURN!

|   | A | B | C | D | E | F |
|---|---|---|---|---|---|---|
| 1 |   |   |   |   |   |   |
| 2 |   |   |   |   |   |   |
| 3 |   |   |   |   |   |   |
| 4 |   |   |   |   |   |   |
| 5 |   |   |   |   |   |   |
| 6 |   |   |   |   |   |   |
| 7 |   |   |   |   |   |   |

A B C D E F
1
2
3
4
5
6
7

# YOUR TURN!

|   | A | B | C | D | E | F |
|---|---|---|---|---|---|---|
| 1 |   |   |   |   |   |   |
| 2 |   |   |   |   |   |   |
| 3 |   |   |   |   |   |   |
| 4 |   |   |   |   |   |   |
| 5 |   |   |   |   |   |   |
| 6 |   |   |   |   |   |   |
| 7 |   |   |   |   |   |   |

A B C D E F

# YOUR TURN!

|   | A | B | C | D | E | F |
|---|---|---|---|---|---|---|
| 1 |   |   |   |   |   |   |
| 2 |   |   |   |   |   |   |
| 3 |   |   |   |   |   |   |
| 4 |   |   |   |   |   |   |
| 5 |   |   |   |   |   |   |
| 6 |   |   |   |   |   |   |
| 7 |   |   |   |   |   |   |

A B C D E F
1
2
3
4
5
6
7

# YOUR TURN!

|   | A | B | C | D | E | F |
|---|---|---|---|---|---|---|
| 1 |   |   |   |   |   |   |
| 2 |   |   |   |   |   |   |
| 3 |   |   |   |   |   |   |
| 4 |   |   |   |   |   |   |
| 5 |   |   |   |   |   |   |
| 6 |   |   |   |   |   |   |
| 7 |   |   |   |   |   |   |

A B C D E F
1
2
3
4
5
6
7

# YOUR TURN!

|   | A | B | C | D | E | F |
|---|---|---|---|---|---|---|
| 1 |   |   |   |   |   |   |
| 2 |   |   |   |   |   |   |
| 3 |   |   |   |   |   |   |
| 4 |   |   |   |   |   |   |
| 5 |   |   |   |   |   |   |
| 6 |   |   |   |   |   |   |
| 7 |   |   |   |   |   |   |

|     | A | B | C | D | E | F |
|-----|---|---|---|---|---|---|
| 1   |   |   |   |   |   |   |
| 2   |   |   |   |   |   |   |
| 3   |   |   |   |   |   |   |
| 4   |   |   |   |   |   |   |
| 5   |   |   |   |   |   |   |
| 6   |   |   |   |   |   |   |
| 7   |   |   |   |   |   |   |

# YOUR TURN!

|   | A | B | C | D | E | F |
|---|---|---|---|---|---|---|
| 1 |   |   |   |   |   |   |
| 2 |   |   |   |   |   |   |
| 3 |   |   |   |   |   |   |
| 4 |   |   |   |   |   |   |
| 5 |   |   |   |   |   |   |
| 6 |   |   |   |   |   |   |
| 7 |   |   |   |   |   |   |

A B C D E F
1
2
3
4
5
6
7

# YOUR TURN!

|   | A | B | C | D | E | F |
|---|---|---|---|---|---|---|
| 1 |   |   |   |   |   |   |
| 2 |   |   |   |   |   |   |
| 3 |   |   |   |   |   |   |
| 4 |   |   |   |   |   |   |
| 5 |   |   |   |   |   |   |
| 6 |   |   |   |   |   |   |
| 7 |   |   |   |   |   |   |

A B C D E F
1
2
3
4
5
6
7

# YOUR TURN!

|   | A | B | C | D | E | F |
|---|---|---|---|---|---|---|
| 1 |   |   |   |   |   |   |
| 2 |   |   |   |   |   |   |
| 3 |   |   |   |   |   |   |
| 4 |   |   |   |   |   |   |
| 5 |   |   |   |   |   |   |
| 6 |   |   |   |   |   |   |
| 7 |   |   |   |   |   |   |